Her
Peace
of
Mind

Huldah Shlomit Dauid

Thoughts, Poems, & Encouragement

Royal Roots | California

Copyright © 2020 by Huldah Dauid

All rights reserved. No part of this publication may be reproduced, distributed or transmitted in any form or by any means, without prior written permission.

Huldah Dauid/Royal Roots
www.HerRoyalRoots.com

Book Layout © 2017 BookDesignTemplates.com

Her Peace of Mind/ Huldah Dauid. -- 1st ed.
ISBN 978-1-7337520-3-9

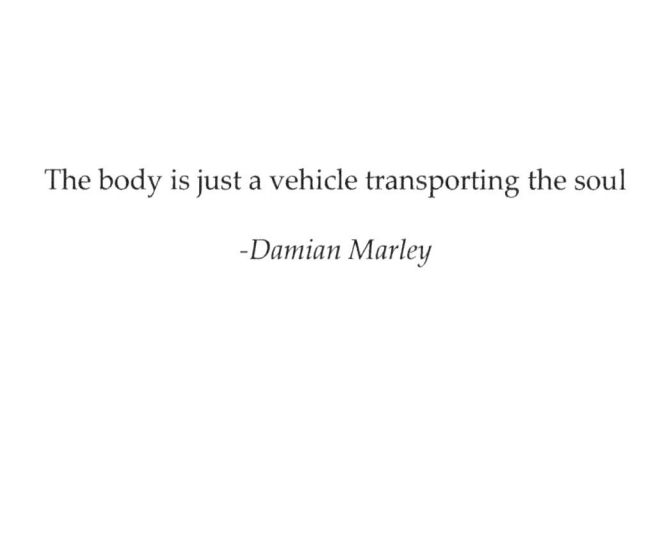

The body is just a vehicle transporting the soul

-Damian Marley

Foreword

Her

Her love for the people is awe inspiring
Her hope for an expected end is a reminder
that Yah will finish the work that He has
started within you
Her family is everything
Her writing is a gift, enjoy and cherish it
Her presence will flow from generation to
generation, like waves that continue to meet
the sea shore

Peace

There's peace in those waves tumultuous
tides
There's peace in the unknown
There's peace found in the stories of my dear
friends writing
Peace is found in the perfecting process

Of

Of all the people I have met in life
Of all the experiences I have ever had

Of all the conversations I've participated in
Of all the words that have peaked my interest
Of them all, hers have been the most impactful, influential, and inspiring
Of them all

Mind

Her mind is an archive of the ancients
Her mind is her greatest weapon
Her mind, her most beautiful attribute
Her mind she shares with you all

I pray that you all find שלום
Through her words in
Her Peace of Mind

Your dearest friend,
Lauren NeFesha

the journey is full of peaks and valleys
but provisions
have been made
for your successful completion

all you have to do is take the first step

You know brains can talk if everybody be quiet

(My 4 year old)

I'm not always mad at you
sometimes my frustration is confused with anger
maybe its birthed from the abyss that keeps me
from you
you see, I am frustrated
because
you don't feel the same disappointment I feel
when we are out of alignment
when it is wrong...
all I want to do is make it right

sisterhood is likened to the pages of a journal.
It holds your deepest fears, anxieties, and traumas
but also captures your greatest accomplishments and victories
I am here to celebrate you in confidence, guard your secrets, and nudge you toward who Yah wants you to be.

arms raised
vines exposed
take what is barren
so that I can bear good fruit
kind and gentle gardener
have your way

(Pruning)

Yah help me get to a place
Where humbling experiences
are not humiliating

Where being brought low
 is not depressing

Where being pruned
doesn't leave me feeling naked

Yah help me to find comfort in your shadow
and make the presence of your glory
        even in affliction
            a place of serenity

Yah take me to your hidden place
Where I can learn of your mysteries

Take me to a quiet place
Remind me of your complex simplicity

When the perils of life overwhelm me
            Hide me

The Adversary comes to remind you
 of your past, so you give up on your future.

The Adversary plants
 lying seeds in a fruitful field
he wants people to doubt the crop.

The Adversary's last ditch effort
 is to try and kill your witness
he knows that you are powerful
and with Torah you are untouchable.

Know that you are invincible until your task is complete

THE DISTRACTION IS AN ILLUSION

The Adversary cannot touch the body so he wars in the mind

Never forget

that the Hebrew court of popular opinion
rebelled against Moses

voted not to go into the promise land

killed the Messiah

and told them to put the blood on us

If you can't use your discernment with all the
evidence on the table.

I don't know what you want me to say.

(explaining attacks)

while in the midst of serious internal growth
respect your need to rest

(Burn out)

Behave wisely in the midst of your frenemies
They fear your focus

void of writing but the tension is thick
mood set, tempo undancable
I hate this techno vibe

fumbling over easy words
like please, thank you, and I understand
struggling with pride to say things like I need
your help and I miss you.

blank slate
blank stare
shoulder shrugs and I don't care(s)

    Build up

time that once flew by now drags
clocks watched for moments to flee from tension
did I forget to mention
there is constant dissension

keeping tally in invisible writing
want to speak but no words
how did we move from cotton candy clouds
to rejection, deflection, and separation by these
crowded thoughts
I thought
we said
    Blank Slate

The greatest self-care is soul care
& service to Yah

when I saw you
I saw a fire
I mistook it for passion
but it was a wild and untamed
seeking my very breathe
you consumed me

(wild fire)

how is it that you have become my enemy
the one who lays down next to me
knows the most intimate parts of me
yet can't seem to feel my energy

if I'm not connected to you
then am I even human
what's wrong with me
unlovable
punished

you confuse my faith
because if this is my fate
then does God really even care about me
your distance is a reflection
 of my lack of divine connection

an accessory
secluded
so no one has access to me
FUCK this I'm confused, helpless
this SHIT should be simple
but now all I am doing is second guessing me

come please and make me free

Somebody

some of earths greatest jewels
are stored in the cracked and destitute
grounds of distant lands

It reminds me of you

{Abandoned}
                Wild

                        B r o k e n

yet full of treasure
the only task is to seek it out
look past the tough & dry exterior
I'm invested
only having one expectation
that you understand the richness
beneath your uncultivated soil.

[Hardpan]

I am afraid of the future
hoping leads to disappointment
anticipation to degradation
preparation sees to culminate
in the theft of stored joy

while I know standing firm in the now
is merely a statuesque figure
being propelled forward through time
unresponsive and inanimate

                        Still is safe.

while time may pass me by
while I may never gain
I am positive
that with feet planted
nothing can be taken or lost

                  I will just mourn the time.

I.

She's shy
she learned
to hide in her safe place long ago
tucked away
in a world where
hurt
fear
anger
and disappointment
could not reach her

She's bold
in her set apart space
she rehearses the words
she would use to change the world
She dreams of becoming a lawyer
to free her father from prison
and a psychologist to heal
the generational curses
that plague her community

She's scared
after spending so much time
in this secluded space
she has realized that the possibility
of emerging seems less and less likely
she tells herself "it's safe here and no one will
miss what they have never known"

she makes her retreat her home.

She's curious
after many years locked away
she meets a man with fire in his eyes
and decides maybe there is refuge there
so she decides to peek out
as she emerges slowly
from her place of security and safety
moving toward the warmth
of his fiery gaze

                    he goes cold
                        ICE COLD
the type of cold that's so cold it feels hot

she stays awhile to sort things out
but hypothermic and frost bitten
she drags her frozen soul
to a garden of weeds
neglected because of a futile journey.

She's repairing
in her garden
she slowly begins to nurture and weed yearning
for a small resemblance
of what once was
she replants and weeds
replants and whispers
replants and nurtures her refuge back
to an even grander state than before

she decides she won't ever leave again
the repairing was exhausting

She's at peace
the girl inside
looks like a woman on the outside
she experiences the world through her eyes
      "I am whole. Let them in."

II.

a kindred spirit emerges
the girl on the inside tugs on my heart strings

"you see her she knows pain, she knows
disappointment, but look closer, the sun dances
in her eyes, there's light inside, and if there is
light there is a garden, and if there is a garden
maybe there is a little girl like me. "

maybe she will come and play.
maybe she will skip through tall grasses
and blow dandelions.
maybe she will laugh
and tell jokes while skipping rocks.
maybe she will stay
just a little while
maybe she will remind me little girls can still be
little girls.
maybe, just maybe, she will make me brave
enough to show the world what I'm really made
of.

In the white noise and early mornings
is where I find you
tucked away in delayed sunrises
and prolonged hours of nothingness
you reside in the stillness of solitude
the place where each inhale and exhale
of my borrowed breath can be heard
I am present in this moment
I thought you would never return

        Hello Silence,
        So grateful you have come home

today I am irritable.
I am impatient
time seems to move too fast
and I can't keep up
blocking up my time and trying to focus
knowing there is more to my day
than what I presently partake in
I feel like a failure today
I don't want to do anything

(counterproductive)

a different kind of beautiful
Like snow
covering the mountains
Like parted skin
on the hips, thighs, and belly of a woman
who has loaned her body to bring life
Like honey
melting into warm tea after a long day
Like how you throw your head back
and clinch your gut
while laughing
Like warm tears
streaming down your face
when you are free
Like the still and quiet
when you know, finally
it is well with my soul

yesterday I had a thought
about being in limbo.
not being who I used to be
and fully despising that person
but not exactly understanding
who I am supposed to be
and through lack of understanding despising
that person as well
I felt caught
between identities
feeling and not ever truly understanding
what I am.
who am I?

then I realized
that as long as I am seeking my identity apart
from the one who created me
then I will always be questioning and doubtful.

so I am consciously making a choice

                to choose YAH

two things cannot occupy the same space
at the same time.
America is the overseer
to make sure that the Hebrews
don't go back home
that is their part in the confederacy.

Hebrews
the only nation of captives
 still in land of captivity after captivity

even animals get released back into their natural environment
when do we return

but someone is occupying the land so now there is nowhere to go

I tried to manipulate and control people
I harbored resentment
I wanted to be forgiven
but I wouldn't forgive others.

If you don't master your emotions
the adversary will use your emotions to become
your master.

buried trauma will become your trigger
triggers are the adversary's play ground

If your mind wanders in prayer
stop and pray about that
In doing so you will pray
without ceasing

I am bare before you
array me in your brilliance
so I might shine forth
as the light of the world
drawing men and women to you

the unknown is a fertile void

I have lost the joy of my salvation

(shattered)

Through the turmoil of trial I have tarried
50 days in the belly of despair
wreathing with the pain
of betrayal and discomfort
I have waited

Seek thee early you said, but why have you hidden yourself?
ask and receive, but what have you taken?
knock and you will answer
OH! How did I end up outside of the door?

Reveal to me
please no longer conceal from me
the joy of my salvation

Descend like a dove
or even with the fury of a dark cloud
that awaits her opportunity to break forth
and sends a trembling frequency through my bones.

Come for me as you have so many times before
rescue me with your mighty right hand
my arms are lifted like a child
mount me on your wings
and transport me to a safe place
brood over me
nurture me within your bosom.

O Yah my Elohim come for me lest my faith slip.
circle round about me
lest the adversary see my mortal wound
comfort me lest this grieving, lost, and wayward
soul succumb to the inner me.

save me
from me
I am waiting

(A Psalm in HD)

The grave is not my resting place
because my beginning is not from the darkness
of the grave
my source is from the Everlasting Light

Job 17:15

I'm tired of breaking *HIS* heart

what is man that you are mindful of him?

my life, my breathe, my testament, my fame, my character is expressed in man. When you have invested love you nurture it

(apple of HIS eye)

today I sat and watched his love raise her blood pressure.

(Echad) comes when two are one.

their R.A.W unity intertwined fighting for her life

hoping love tips the balance against the odds of death

I see you
through you
I notice light in your eyes
I can see when you hide behind the veil of your soul

I catch the frustration in your inflection when you want to go but don't know the direction

I ידע Yada. I know

I noticed you during the coldest winter
barren and leafless
what caught my eye was the birds
that nestled in your branches
they seemed to know of a refuge that I could not see

The bees that made sweet honey in your inward parts. They trusted your rugged structure to protect their queen.
your trunk held the etching of a thousand lovers and the weight of their love didn't move you.
I saw the promise of your stability in the sureness of your roots.

all these signs of life confirmed what couldn't be seen on the surface would soon manifest. With divine vision. With wisdom. I knew you would bloom

when spring arrives and newness is ushered in. I remembered. The promise. The shadow to come, and now look at you. FLOURISHING.

like the gravitational pull of the moon
forces the seed in the soil
to show forth her tender plant
 giving sign of fruit that will be borne.

the full moon of the feast is pulling on the soil of my heart and forcing his word to come forth and my seeds to sprout in order to be judged.

Yahuah almighty prune and snatch out the parts of me that are not from you and nurture the set apart portion.

the ground is my kinswoman
In her resides purpose and power
she nourishes
she is a sure foundation
she is life
she teaches me about bringing forth fruit

                in due season

a space with no boundaries is truly open
scattered pieces, jagged edges, separated
individual pieces of a former wholeness waiting
for the great mosaic master to repurpose the
fragmented into a masterpiece
is there anything with more potential than a
broken heart

> raw material awaiting its wholeness
> there is nothing more whole than a
> shattered heart

being able to witness
someone at their lowest
is more than a moment to observe
it's an opportunity to build them back
toward worship and their call

I need a...

Every version of you is my favorite version, kind of love.

An awaiting of my arrival, like a bride
on her wedding day
EVERYDAY
                kind of love.

Transition is just an opportunity to evolve with me
                kind of love.

That head over hills
 peering into the next dimension

KIND OF LOVE

(needy)

When you are loved
Let it be
Don't let the feelings of inadequacy blur the reality:

That YOU, in all you imperfections
DESERVE
the filter of PERFECTION
that my LOVE for you
CREATES

There's an *appointment*
on the other side of your *disappointment*

passing

from one version of myself

to the next

(emerging)

the constant struggle to merge dualities is
intense because the depth of your unmanaged
trauma determines the intensity of your duality

farming is in my nature because I am earth
Seeds planted in expectation
nourished in compassion
blossomed by divine ordinance
turned and tilled
the process and restoration
complete
whether dormant or prolifically bearing
I am always in season

melodically laced through instruments
orchestrated to reach the ears of a beloved
men and women risking all earthly wealth
because there is no equivalent thereof
Oh love!

commanded and imperative
the verb the Creator uses
to express his essence & majesty
That's love!

unequivocally expressed
captivating, stimulating
stronger than any drug
addicted to love!

rare but available in the hearts of those that
believe in it.
lost but until found
I'm feening it
if it's not this, then it's not love!

heads suspended in the clouds
feet off the ground
Alice in Wonderland
rabbit hole
lost in the abyss of this
Love!

through the dark alleys, twists and turns
of what seems to be a rabbit hole you lead me
like the Cheshire cat to wonderland

you begin early priming my mind
with bent knees and HalleluYah's. A voice
uplifted like the cry of an eagle in her glory
Your devotion captivated me

Your bags are full of books of distant lands
your shelves of writings meant to plunge
even the deepest thinker
into unknown depths
saturated
I return only for breaths

going deeper and deeper into dark unknowns
that require feeling and sensing
without optical vision
you must look with you heart

your exploration
causes my inward parts to turn
staring in your eyes I see your wheels whirling
like a grandfather clock
every gear working toward the unfolding
of times greatest mysteries
sometimes I stare into your eyes
hypnotized by the intricate coiling
and disentangling of every complex thought

I have seen neurons fire and new synaptic
pathways form before my eyes.

looking at you is like looking out into space
knowing that what I see is only the surface of
untamed and uncharted vast unknowness

You are light years away even in the same space
what brings you back to earth
and makes you tangible
is when you speak.

your words have a cadence and a frequency
that reminds me of the heart beating in my chest
when you are revealing your thoughts
mountains to peak
trees to lower their branches
lions to purr like kittens
The conviction in which you speak
the way your lips part
allowing the ancient wisdom to pass through
causes my breath to rise and fall
like I have run a marathon
my brain pants as it tries to keep pace
my brain quivers as you take it on a journey time
traveling and sitting at the feet sages and
philosophers
My cerebral function is in overdrive
downloading endless stories and poetry

that inspires me to pour forth like water, divine wisdom, mixed with liberating sweet undertones I have become a fountain bursting forth like a spring of living water in the desert.
You have made me your oasis.
A place holding sweet water for the next weary traveler.

I now stand beaconing at the rabbit hole. Eyes ablaze. Explore with me the depths and the heights.

If we were in cotton fields with whip to back
and hand to plow
It would be your distant song
carried by the wind
 that would keep me sane

If we were in sugar cane fields
on the humid islands
it would be the remembrance in the breeze
of how we swayed
to the beat of the African drums
that would encourage my heart

If we stole from our homes
placed beneath ships
on a voyage to a distant land
it would be the thought of a tomorrow
and the anticipation of redemption
that would force us to get it right this time

what does it mean to be inspired?
To have the gentle whisper of the Infinite One
tell you it's the wrong time
to tap out and get tired.

Is it the gentle country breeze on a hot day
reminding you that connected to the land
is where you are called to be?

or could it be a weary traveler from a distant
land carrying only her soul
and the gift of an open heart
ready and willing
for another long journey ahead.

what inspires the uninspired
will we ever know?

but what I do know
is that every time
we connect by phone or in person
 you remind me
of the infinite that resides within me
You see me
You care
You make it possible
to find joy in the simple things
to seek the creator in ways
that in aforetime
only existed on pages of ancient text

Your love is a simple seed of hope planted in the midst of my doubtful stony heart
Your commitment
is the accountability I need to grow, so...

Uproot with me
Plant fruit with me
Relax with me
Reboot with me
Purge these westernized minds and bear fruit with me.

Then walk with me
 even after this finite position of time and space
to that eternal place
where we will serve at the Fathers feet
laughing and crying
under healing trees telling

  how
       we
              made
                    it
                          over.

Inheritance vs generational curses

What are you preparing and passing down?

death
the nagging reminder
of the impermanence of life

it leaves a feeling of void
which seems to linger without hope.

but death is also
the connection and collection of broken hearts
scattered throughout the universe
seeking home and wholeness
in tear blurred gazes and lingering hugs
embraces from those who have felt it's sting
and will one day journey into its irreversible
embrace

as I sit in the cemetery
looking at others who have lost
seeing them stare into the soulless void
of full graves
I too, am reminded
of the way all things go
I am connected to them, and their pain
although felt through different circumstances
their pain is one with mine

we are whole
because of our collective brokenness
once this is realized
we can be a vehicle for collaborative healing

It is possible what one perceives can be substantially different from objective reality

I'm never going to make it easy
I will push you
Because sometimes a push

                    and a free *fall*

are the recipe a winged beauty needs to
actualize her infinite potential

                    and *FLY*

you watched me drown
because saving me
would require
getting wet
by the raging waters
you created.

-risk

return
because the fear of your wrath upon arrival is
better
than the eerie silence
of your absence .

coming back to you
is anxiety coupled with bad decisions
descending from heights
only to fall into dark clouds and rain storms
you wait for me
      my dark place
      my dreary drizzle
      my slice of insanity
oh how I wish
I could keep my head
above the melancholy clouds of despair
I must self-talk
to keep from drowning
in the water of my crying soul

remember
re-member
re-mem-ber
I chant silently

remember
that just above
the precipitation
is elevation

heights with lights
visions and sights
unobstructed views
Fight to fly
      fight   to   FLY!

the sorrow of conception being multiplied is so that the woman can understand just how much it took for Yah to perfect something. Because she didn't have to toil, she didn't understand the gift

the same is true of man. He didn't know what it took for Yahuah to create a place like Eden. For him to appreciate the gift, he had to take on the responsibility of cultivating it.

what great rejoicing is had once mankind knows what it takes on a small human scale to do the magnificent works of Yahuah.

every seed I have brought forth
has been in sorrow
I guard you in my womb and fear your loss
my body has been hardened to protect
but I am soft for you
they don't see your worth or your potential
those who see the potential fear you

Don't shrink
Don't miscarry
Don't let the burden
cause you
to come to me
still born

Elohim guard the promise
that you have called me to carry.

(guard it)

My ancestors survived the Trail of Tears. They were released during slavery and kept our history as a precious jewel for such a time as this. Your ancestor is Harriet Tubman, who freed her mind and those of countless men and women. I come from freedom fighters in Madagascar who, with a female queen, fought off colonial oppression. You come from freedom farmers who saw the importance of land and generational wealth. Tell me it wasn't the divine influence of the Infinite One that made us friends. We were knit together through generations of cries and moans that resonated into the wombs of our mothers and then nourished by the mammary of their individual oppression. We were the children tucked tight in the arms of women, not seeing a way out whispering to our souls with vibrations and fears to free them. We have a responsibility, and as I sit on a porch in a rocking chair, I am given a glimpse of a tomorrow when peace is birth out of ancestral chains being broken by unbreakable women seeking amendment in the right now.

(friends for a cause)

Setting free the parts of me
that no longer exists
responding to the heart song
 I resist
yet persists

(calling)

sex is supposed to awaken
the softer side of a woman
it causes her to blossom

how can a woman be
a tender delicate flower
vulnerable
soft
submissive
if she is handled harshly

as the weaker vessel
handle me with care

how would you feel if I opened up and exposed
your deepest parts
then trampled over you

don't cause the lotus to bloom
with hopes of perpetual sunshine
only to push it back
under the murky waters
If you don't have any intention
of keeping the flower in bloom
don't cultivate the soil!

(wounded daughter of Zion)

lost does not mean forgotten
it means not in its proper place

we are not lost
we are just out of our proper place.

(lost tribes)

racism was created
in order to aid
in replacement of Yah's people

the observation isn't wrong
it's the misapplication of what is observed
 that is dangerous.

If children must obey their father
then it is even more true
that we as children of YHWH
must obey HIM

(child-like)

fighting bitterness
everyday it's a struggle
I can be haughty
I have a slick tongue.
But how does acting
in my on strength benefit the kingdom

I'm am supposed to be silent
let Yah fight my battles
But what happens
when being silent
doesn't work

obedience comes from the heart first. whatever is
in your heart
will determine what you believe
finally, what you believe
will determine how you behave.

(but first, obedience)

In order for a caterpillar
 to turn into a butterfly
it has to be a caterpillar
 and not a moth.

(Yoshiyahu)

If (*you*) want something (*said*)

the way (*you*) want to (*hear*) it

say it yourself

I am on a journey

Destination						Unknown

but there is a wisdom in not knowing

(Trusting the Process)

If thy trauma is epigenetic;
THEN...
so shall thy healing be also!

Breaking Generational Curses 24:7

I moved and packed boxes
   I relocated but I brought baggage

I moved but carried the contents from the
   old house with me

I bought a new house but have foolishly
   packed the memory of the old one

I am unpacking. Making new places
   familiar.

I am unpacking and finding myself
   surrounded by what I moved away from.

weed seeds are already in the soil.

>when you cultivate good soil you are also going to water the weeds

be prepared

sisterhood exists because the need for nurturing is eternal.

those who nurture must be nurtured

> those who heal must have a safe place to break and be redesigned

those who are strong must have space to soften and let their guards down.

> those who birth must find the womb of sisterhood as a place to actualize the many gifts bestowed upon her.

sisterhood exists because we are life givers and her/she/us/OUR wholeness are important to femininity and true divinity.

I'm just venting.
I had an internal meltdown today!
I have "just one of those days on repeat."

Sometimes I wonder if this is the right decision. If my children were at school all day then I could get so much done. I feel like their educational development depends on me and some days are inconsistent. I am not teaching them in a traditional way and I would love to plan better. I am trying to get up early to do everything and every day I seem to fall short. I am drowning and the thought of not getting things done makes me just stop ugh! But tomorrow is a new day.

(free day)

Feminine without fear

(1 Peter 3:6)

Huldah resides in California. Her passion and focus is the liberation of women and children through truth of their rich cultural heritage.

Made in the USA
Monee, IL
21 November 2020